PUEBLO

by Marie Richards

HOUGHTON MIFFLIN

BOSTON

This is the Taos Pueblo in New Mexico. The Taos Pueblo Indians live here. They have lived here for over 1,000 years.

Tradition is important in the Pueblo.
Things are almost as they always have been.
There is no running water or electricity.

People still bake bread in clay ovens. People create crafts in the old ways.

People speak the old language.
Some wear the clothes of long ago.

Some stories are told and retold.
Pueblo people perform dances on special
ceremony days.

Young children go to
the Pueblo school. They
learn about the old ways.

Many visitors come to the Pueblo.
They learn about the culture or ways
of the Taos Pueblo Indians.